Flowers in Folk Art

Jacques Zuidema

Introduction 3
Materials and requirements 4
Sanding, base painting and tracing patterns 5
Simple painting techniques 7
Advanced painting techniques 8
Daffodil, zinnia and iris 11
Assendelfter rose, tiger lily and tulip 15
Summer rose, honeysuckle and anemone 19
Chest of drawers, trinket box and blue tray 21
Butler's trays, document box and serving tray 23
Tidy box, pale pink serving tray and wall plaque 25
Birds 27
Crackling and antiquing 29
Red robins 31
Finishing, cleaning and maintenance 32

Kangaroo Press

Introduction

Before I explain the techniques used in Assendelfter painting, I would like to give you a little historical background to this uniquely decorative form of folk art.

Assendelft is a small place in the Zaanstreek (near Amsterdam) where at the beginning of this century a number of beautifully decorated old chests, tables and other pieces of furniture were discovered. They originally came from Amsterdam around the first half of the 17th century. At that time this type of work was known as Assendelvers; it was made by whiteworkers who worked with a white timber in contrast to their colleagues, who used beautiful pieces of pine and mahogany. The whiteworkers needed permission from the Painters' Guild and the elders of the council of Amsterdam to make this beautiful furniture. The official permission documents have been preserved to this day.

As well as the exquisite biblical scenes found on the door panels (but not shown in this book), the furniture was decorated with festive flower arrangements, a wonderful world of jasmine, roses, spring blossoms, tulips. Even folding tables and wooden wall panels were adorned with these floral motifs.

One of the most important Assendelfter-style painters at that time was the artist Jochem de Vries, who in 1772 was a member of the Amsterdam Painters' Guild.

For a better appreciation of this North Holland decorated whitewood furniture style, it is important to realise that the paler woods would have been cheaper than pine or mahogany. However, because the whitewood was softer, a lot of the furniture has been lost.

Some of the original work was painted in casseine or tempera, but these pieces were quite rare. Most of the furniture that has been preserved and displayed in museums in Arnhem, Enkhuisen and Zaandijk, was painted with oil paints.

< *Blue chest of drawers, oval blue serving tray with zinnias, oval green trinket box; see page 21 for patterns*

The development of the Assendelfter designs has a correlation with the evolving flower growing industry of the Netherlands. This can be seen by the gradual development of different sorts of tulips. These were very carefully reproduced in order to be botanically correct. Similar care was taken in painting the General de Wett tulip, the anemones, irises, zinnias and jasmine flowers. These flower motifs were often combined with birds such as robins and bluebirds.

As a pioneer of the recently revived Assendelfter style, I have allowed myself the artistic licence of adding some typical present-day Dutch flowers to the classic motifs, bringing a more modern vision to this antique decorative painting style.

I have tried to present the richness of traditional Assendelfter flower paintings in this book, but I hope that a little of the original technique will become a part of everyone's craft. I wish you many hours of intense pleasure with this hobby.

Jacques Tuidema
Decorative Painter

Bouquet of gerberas, daisies, ranunculi and cornflowers, painted using mainly large and small daisy strokes

Materials and requirements

This photograph shows a range of folk art requirements available from good hobby and craft shops. Not all these articles are essential to make a start. I recommend both a large and small round synthetic fibre brush (size 8 or 10 and a size 3 or 4).

Folk art paints are available in a wide variety of containers—metal tubes, squeezable plastic tubes, glass jars, etc. The plastic tubes are very handy as the paint rarely dries out. Six basic colours should be sufficient to start; red, citrus yellow, medium blue, dark brown, leaf green and white or ivory.

There is a huge selection of antique tints (base paints), in different brands and colours. Always remember to wash the brushes thoroughly after painting. Use water and detergent; the brush should be carefully squeezed and dried with a small piece of cotton fabric.

1 Acrylic paint in glass jars with screw on lids (Marabu, Wacofin, Decorfin)
2 Acrylic paint in plastic tubes (DecoArt, Delta, FolkArt)
3 Acrylic paint in metal tubes; more pigment concentrate (Permalba, Talens, Rowney, Winsor & Newton)
4 Acrylic paint in small sample pots (Talens, Wacofin, Marabu)
5 Base paint in large plastic containers (Delta, FolkArt, DecoArt)
6 Base paint in large tubes (Lefranc & Bourgeois, Pebeo de France)
7 Acrylic paint medium; assists in paint flow (Talens, Winsor & Newton)
8 Brushes made from synthetic and bristle hair
9 Sponge applicators
10 Casseine-emulsion paint for fine detail and line work (Tamma)
11 Rubber gloves (for base painting and antiquing)
12 Water soluble antiquing agent (DecoArt)
13 Jars of antiquing agent needing turpentine for thinning (Talens)
14 Quick drying oil paint medium to speed the antiquing process (Winsor & Newton, Talens)
15 Flat plate to use as a palette for antiquing
16 Lint-free cotton fabric
17 White or coloured chalk for tracing designs
18 Tracing or tissue paper 50–80 g for tracing patterns
19 Ballpoint pen with a fine point for tracing
20 Large and samll hogshair brushes, widths 10–15 mm ($^3/_8$"–1")
21 Wooden paint stirrers
22 Small paint roller for base paints
23 Piece of timber for sampling colours
24 Stirring sticks for the small jars of acrylic paint
25 Storage container for base paints
26 Crackling medium (FolkArt, DecoArt)

Sanding, Base Painting and Tracing Patterns

Sanding and Base Painting

Base painting simply means preparing and painting an object to give it a coloured base on which to paint the design.

Timber surfaces need to be free from dust and grease before painting begins.

New timber: this usually only needs a light sanding with a piece of fine sandpaper. Any uneven marks or holes in the timber can be filled with wood putty, which can be sanded when dry. A water soluble wood sealer can also be used. This is quick-drying and fills in any marks. Lightly sand between coats.

Old timber: wash the object in lukewarm water till clean and leave to dry. Once dry, it is easier to make a judgement on the condition of the wood. Always sand very carefully.

Be very careful when using acid-based products. Always read the instructions first. If an object is very dirty or greasy it can be cleaned with a gentle detergent, methylated spirits or washing soda. Sand the article before painting it with a primer and base coat. Two thin coats of base paint give a very good effect.

You could try the new acrylic primer, (a water-based primer from Talens of Trimetal). Gesso can also be used as a base for timber, canvas and paper.

Articles made of ivory or plain cardboard can be coated with Gesso, then coated with a water-thinned coat of acrylic medium. This is a good base for painting.

When the object has been coated with a good base coat you are ready to begin painting.

Tracing Patterns

In this book you will find patterns for the flower arrangements pictured. These can be enlarged or reduced on a photocopier to whatever size best suits you.

I do not recommend carbon paper for tracing the patterns, as it sometimes leaves marks. Use chalk and a good quality tissue paper; I have found this to be the easiest way.

Trace the pattern with a fine felt tip or ball point pen or HB pencil (illustration A). Turn the tissue paper over and run the chalk across the pattern from left to right (illustration B), always working in the same direction. Use your finger tips to rub the chalk into the pores of the paper. Blow the excess chalk from the paper. Turn the pattern over and position it on the object to be painted. It's a good idea to attach the pattern with a bit of masking tape. With a fine pencil or ball point pen as a stylus, follow the lines on the paper and press down onto the object (illustration C).

When the tracing paper is removed you should see the clean lines of the design (illustration D). The pattern can be removed later with a piece of clean cloth.

The use of purple, blue or white carbon paper is not recommended.

A. The design is traced onto the object with a fine-tipped ball point pen

B. Running the chalk firmly across the design on the back of the tissue paper

C. Placing the paper with the chalk side down on top of the object; the lines are traced with a pen

D. The result shows the chalk lines on the object

Simple painting techniques

The following simple brush strokes are the bases of many designs. Practise them often and your painting technique will constantly improve.

1. Stem stroke
Use a No. 6 or No. 8 brush. Before picking up the brush, practise resting your hand on your ring finger and little finger. Totally relax your arm and hand. Check your normal writing posture.

With well-shaken acrylic paint in a dull colour (brown, black or green), place the brush on the paper and slide it from left to right in thin, even parallel strokes. This stroke will come in handy for the stems of the tulips and anemones as well as the wings of the birds. Practise these strokes carefully.

2. Thin-thick-thin stroke (ttt-stroke)
Instead of the very thin stroke we have been making, we will now slowly exert some pressure on the brush. The bristles on the brush will spread out with the increased pressure and become thin again when the pressure is reduced. The centre of the brush stroke will be the widest; the shape will be like the leaf of a tulip. Let the brush do all the work. It will spring back to finish with a point.

This thin-thick-thin stroke is used for tulip leaves, lily-of-the-valley and the tails of birds. Remember—practise makes perfect!

You can also use a combination of two different colours. First dip the whole brush in the green paint and then just cover the tip in white or yellow; use both these colours to make one stroke (see the last tulip leaf).

3. The broken arrow stroke
Place the relaxed hand on the paper. As in the previous exercise, start with a thin stroke and gradually increase the pressure allowing the bristles to fan out. When the widest point has been reached, lift the brush from the paper. The ending can be rounded or slightly frayed-looking. This stroke is often used in plant and flower designs, as well as in motifs using birds (see cornflower on page 6).

4. The contour stroke
Using a No. 4 or No. 6 brush, dip it lightly into the paint. The brush is held vertically. This stroke is almost a form of drawing, with the tip of the brush held firmly between thumb and forefinger. The contour stroke will take a bit of practise. On page 6 this stroke is used for the brown flowers. It's a very important stroke in painting birds and landscapes. Make sure to use a small, even amount of paint.

1. Stem stroke

2. Thin-thick-thin stroke

3. Broken arrow stroke

4. Contour stroke

Stem stroke used to paint tulips

Thin-thick-thin stroke used to paint lily-of-the-valley leaves

Broken arrow stroke used to paint the cornflower leaf

Contour stroke used to paint forget-me-nots

< *Flower bouquet mainly using the brush strokes demonstrated on this page*

Advanced painting techniques

1. Tear drop stroke and its use in painting honeysuckle

2. Comma stroke and its use in painting a crab-apple

3. Flat comma stroke and its use in painting the head and the wings of a bird

For the following slightly more difficult strokes, the same technique applies: practise regularly so that your technique keeps improving and the strokes become more fluid. Next to each demonstrated stroke you will find an example of how it can be used in a simple design.

1. The tear drop stroke (sometimes referred to as the plop stroke). Use your No. 8 synthetic brush to start with. The paint should be well-mixed with a little medium on a palette or a flat plate; the brush should be well covered in paint. Place the brush on the paper and press firmly; pull the brush and lift, making a point at the end to form a tear drop. If you use a No. 10 brush, you can make a larger tear drop. The honeysuckle has been created using a No. 4 brush. You can see that these smaller tear drops have been painted in different directions. This stroke is also used for the centre petal of the tulip.

2. The comma stroke
Using a No. 8 brush with a medium amount of paint, make the shape of a comma. Make a large dot and with a small amount of pressure move the brush either left or right. Practise a few strokes on a smooth piece of paper; face the commas to the left and the right and vary the size.

Comma strokes are used quite often. They are used to make the eyes of birds. On the crab-apple (illustrated) they are used in the upper half of the rounded (apple) shape, with ttt strokes used in the lower half.

3. The flat comma stroke
This is a comma without the large rounded dot at the top. This stroke occurs in roses and the wings of birds. Comma strokes vary widely—some have a fatter dot at the top and some look similar to a C stroke (page 9). Here, the flat comma stroke has been used in the head and the wing of a bird. Practise the large and small comma strokes with a No. 8 brush; eventually you will be able to use a smaller size brush for this stroke. Try and make a nice point at the end. To make smaller commas hold the brush more upright. The flat comma stroke is also used in the centre of the ranunculus (page 21).

4. The S stroke

Making sure the paint has been well shaken or stirred, pick up a small amount of paint with a No. 8 brush. Try and form the letter S a few times, parallel and close together.

Grouping the S strokes together will help you to turn them out better, and make practising easier too. The example of the tulip shows how the S stroke makes a perfect side petal. The tear drop stroke in the centre is added afterwards, straight onto the stem of the tulip.

Use just the one colour to make your practise strokes; later on you will be able to use all the beautiful pastel colours. For the tulip, the brush is double loaded: it is dipped first into red paint, then tipped with a small amount of yellow (see page 15).

5. The C stroke

The C stroke is a little more difficult. Using a good flowing paint draw a large C, starting and ending with the point of the brush. Apply more pressure in the centre of the stroke. The large C stroke is often used to fill in work. The illustration shows the sides of a pomegranate made with two large C strokes. The leaf is a ttt stroke.

6. The moved tear drop stroke

This difficult brush stroke is used not only in painting the iris but also in creating birds and landscape paintings. The background (the iris petal) must have a base colour (in this case, violet or blue) and must be completely dry. Keeping your hand as steady as possible, dip the brush in violet or blue paint, with a small amount of white on the very tip; press the brush down and carefully but quickly move the brush from side to side. Reduce the pressure and finish in a point.

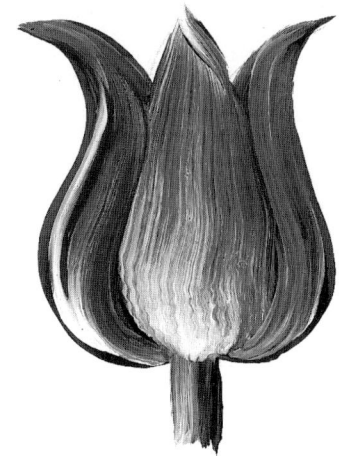

4. The S stroke and its use in painting the side petals of a tulip

5. The C stroke and its use in creating the sides of the pomegranate

6. The moved tear drop stroke and its use in painting an iris

Daffodil, zinnia and iris

After you have practised all the brush strokes, you should be able to paint your first flowers. The bouquet (page 10) consists for the most part of the flowers described below. The unusual daffodil, named 'Salome', has a geranium pink trumpet. In contrast, the iris has been painted in dark colours and the moved tear drop stroke has been used. The bright zinnia is painted in pink and red and there are two different sorts of roses. This bouquet could be used to decorate a wall plaque.

1. Daffodil

A. Begin the centre petal with a large white tear drop stroke; add the side petals with the ttt strokes. The trumpet is white as a base for the yellow. When the paint is dry, paint stem strokes along the edges of the flower in citrus yellow.

B. Paint the whole flower yellow using the stem stroke. The trumpet of the daffodil is painted in cadmium, egg yolk or orange yellow. Using umber and a little sienna, paint a shadow in the still wet trumpet; gently coax the shadow, using only the tip of the brush.

C. Lightly apply yellow over all the petals again. While the surface is still wet, paint in the shadows with a little umber or mid brown (use only a minimum of umber and a little green). Paint some shadows on the trumpet too. Use a green stem stroke for the leaves.

2. The zinnia

A. The first phase is to make a salmon pink base (a tomato shape with a little hole); paint some rough C strokes in two layers

B. The centre hole is painted a carmine red. Dip the brush in carmine red, then in ivory white. Make circular movements with small tear drop strokes on the salmon coloured background.

C. The entire flower is painted over with thinned carmine red (pigment over pigment method), and only at the top are some lighter (white) petals pulled up.

3. The iris

A. The flower petals are all painted in a white base. The outside petals are painted using a slightly bowed ttt stroke; the three upper petals are created using a large tear drop stroke in the centre and two large comma strokes at the sides. The centre petal at the bottom consists of two tear drop strokes painted facing each other. When the paint has dried, paint the lower petals a pale violet.

B. Using the same strokes as before, paint the upper petals a light yellow. The lower petals are painted with a mixture of ultramarine and carmine which results in the dark purple colour shown on the facing page.

C. The upper petals are darkened with sienna and a little orange. Slightly dampen this dark yellow with a little medium; using a large comma stroke with a brush double loaded with citrus yellow and white, apply the specific light effect on the right and left petals.

Accentuate the lower petals by using the moved tear drop stroke. This iris can also be left the darker colour (see page 10) by leaving out the moved tear drop stroke. If you choose to do this, do not draw as many yellow stamens.

1. Building up the yellow daffodil

2. Building up the zinnia

3. Building up the iris

< *A composition with some of the flowers described on this page*

11

Large oval serving tray with zinnias (page 2)

Upper view of green box (page 2)

Side view of green box (page 2)

Assendelfter rose, tiger lily and tulip

These three beautiful flowers are a little more challenging. With the tiger lily you will need to take care with the very strong flat comma strokes. The S stroke is generally the most important stroke in creating the tulip, though it can be done using a two coloured tear drop stroke (see the illustration on cover).

The rose is the typical Assendelfter rose, with the lower half made from ttt strokes and the upper half created using the comma stroke. This rose can be painted in different combinations.

1. Building up the rose

1. The rose
A. The Assendelfter rose has a form similar to a tomato and it is painted using untidy C strokes. Keep the shape more or less circular. Use a No. 8 or No. 10 brush.

B. Paint the centre Bordeaux red. Fill the top half of the rose with comma strokes in red paint tipped with white.

C. Above the centre of the circular form, use large and small comma strokes in a lighter colour. Below the centre, work with ttt strokes (see page 7).

The leaves are painted with a brush double loaded in pine green and yellow.

2. The tiger lily
A. Begin the petals of the lily with white flat comma strokes; do this once or twice over.

B. Using a little watery light brown, paint a teardrop stroke over the white. With brush No. 1 or No. 2, make a row of very fine stamens using carmine red darkened with a little brown.

C. The tiger lily is the yellow variation used on the side of the chest of drawers (page 2). The colours used are cadmium yellow with a little sienna. The stem was created using stem strokes filled in with large comma strokes.

2. Building up the tiger lily

3. Building up the tulip

3. The tulip
A. Use the tear drop stroke from page 8 and the S stroke from page 9 with a No. 8 or No. 10 brush.

B. Begin with the S stroke, using a warm red. Load the brush with red and dip just the tip in the yellow. Make S strokes from top to bottom for the side petals; follow this with a tear drop stroke from bottom to top for the centre petal.

C. The two coloured tear drop stroke for the centre petal begins at the top of the stem. The green stem is made using a stem stroke and the leaf is done with a ttt stroke using a lot of green and some ochre.

< *Assendelfter bouquet with roses, tiger lilies and tulips*

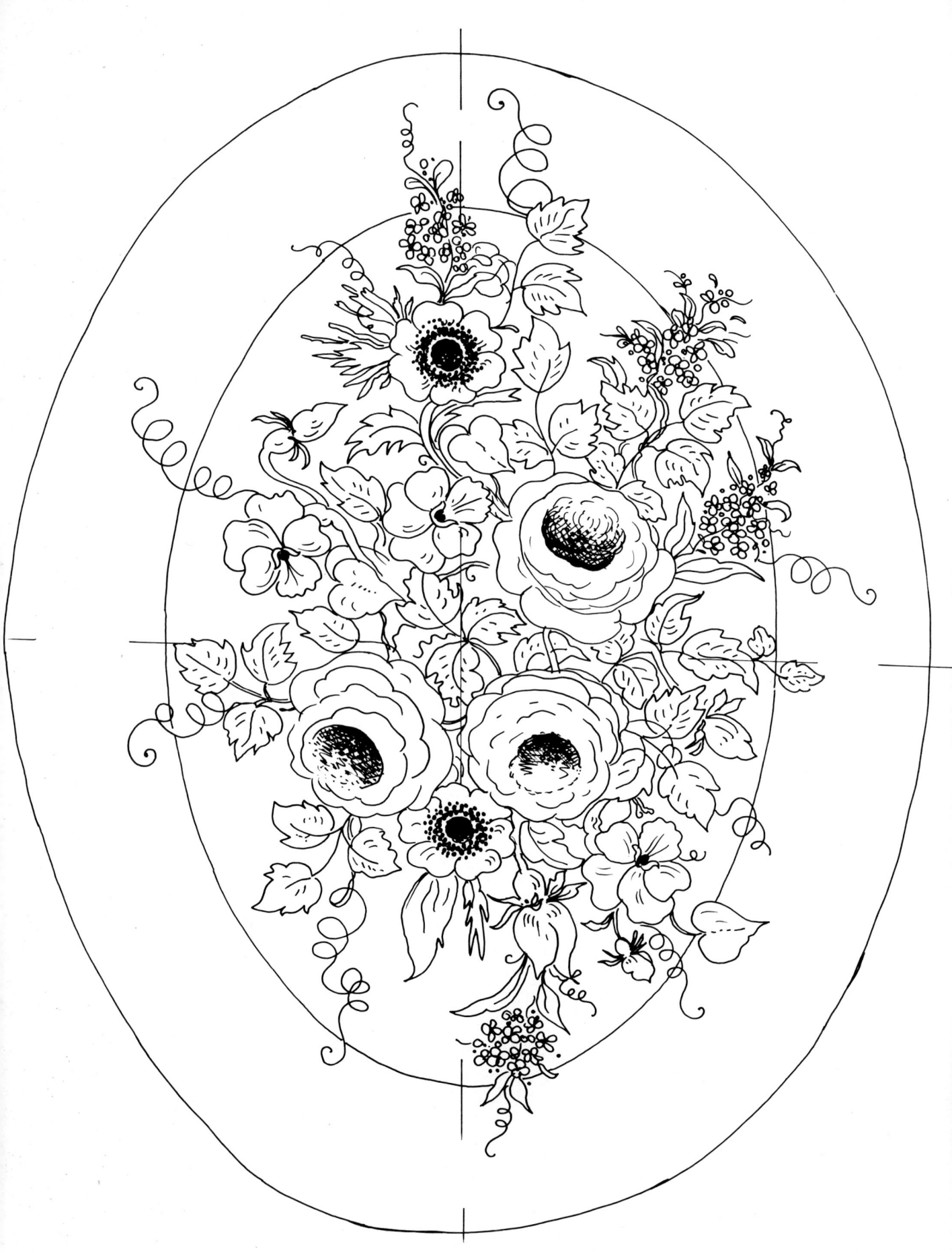

Wall panel with birds, anemones and lily-of-the-valley from page 26
Pale pink serving tray with coral coloured medallion and a composition of summer roses, anemones, pansies and forget-me-nots (page 26)

17

Summer rose, honeysuckle and anemone

The summer rose is a larger, more developed form of the Assendelfter rose, where the outer layer of petals has been applied rather dramatically over the basic apple shape. In this rather advanced creation the brush strokes are made loosely but apart. The very fine honeysuckle provides a lovely contrast. The deep colours of the anemone and the pansy balance the composition.

1. Summer rose
A. The apple shape is circled with three rose petals. Using rough C strokes, paint the base in two layers of ivory white. The oval centre is painted with a little rust brown and the colour is deepened by lightly adding a darker brown.

B. Using a large brush (No. 8 or No. 10), hold the brush flat and lightly shade the apple shape with a little umber. Apply several comma strokes in white. Mix a little mustard yellow or ochre with the white paint.

C. Allow this to dry, then lightly dampen the whole rose with a little acrylic medium. Using a No. 10 brush, cover the top and both sides of the rose with white comma strokes. Ensure that the previously painted shadow is visible here and there.

Remember to use enough paint. The leaves are painted with a No. 8 or No. 10 brush in dark and light green; the veins are given a lighter effect.

2. Honeysuckle
A. You will need to use either a No. 4 or No. 3 brush. It is important to pull the small flat comma stokes towards you as tightly as possible (check the illustration carefully).

B. Tip the end of a brush loaded with white paint with red, pink or orange. Paint the flat comma strokes from different directions, pulling the brush towards you. The stamens are painted in groups of two and three with a No. 1 brush; some small dots are added at the top.

C. The beautiful yellow/orange honeysuckle is made by using a medium red colour tipped with a dark yellow (egg yolk yellow). The stem is made using a stem stroke and a small tear drop stroke coloured mid-green with white.

3. Anemone
A. Create the base of the anemone with two layers of ivory white forming the shape of the petals; this is done by using two short, facing tear drop strokes. The centre is painted black.

B. Using the same strokes, apply two layers of navy blue (lightened with white), over the ivory white base. Dot some stamens around the black centre; then add some more black, plus a few white stamens.

C. Each of the flower petals is lightened with a little white or ivory white. The green leaf is painted with three stem strokes close together and a little white paint to lighten the effect. The leaves give a thread effect.

1. Building up the summer rose

2. Building up the honeysuckle

3. Building up the anemone

< *Bouquet with summer rose, anemone, pansy, honeysuckle and lily-of-the-valley*

Space for a monogram

A
B 
C
D
E 
F

Designs for the blue chest of drawers on page 2 (21 x 15 x 23 cm) (8¼" x 6" x 9")
A. Top motif
B. Left side motif
C. Right side motif
D. Motif from upper drawers
E. Middle drawer motif
F. Lower drawer design

Chest of drawers, trinket box and blue serving tray (page 2)

Chest of drawers

This handy chest of drawers was purchased from a hobby shop. It was a present to my daughter, who now keeps her jewellery in it. It was painted twice with an ivory coloured primer and thoroughly sandpapered. Two coats of pastel blue paint were then applied. Between coats, the chest was lightly rubbed with a fine sandpaper. A silver medallion engraved with her initials was glued to the top and surrounded with a circle of bridal flowers including roses, tulip buds and lilies-of-the-valley. The drawers were decorated with small red roses, ranunculi, tulips and tiger lilies. The two side panels each have a bouquet of flowers pulled together with a silver ribbon. All the drawers have been edged with a grey border; a silver band of 'shimmer silver' from Deco Art has been applied over the grey, using the smallest size sponge.

These designs are very suitable for all sorts of small objects, such as boxes or bouquets on paper (see the patterns opposite).

Ranunculus

This lovely flower is painted as follows:

1. Double load the brush with white and medium blue paint; paint a cross shape with four tear drop strokes. Between these four petals make a second lot of four petals, forming two crosses on top of each other.

2. Make one half of the circle darker by adding a few deep blue tear drop strokes. Paint the protruding centre of the flower with small, flat comma strokes; form the strokes from the outside to the centre, using yellow and white paint. Create a circle of white stamens and draw fine green lines around the outside of the blue petals.

3. Add a few white lines to the centre of the flower. Deepen the colour of some of the petals and gently pull thin white lines over the petals (see pages 2 and 3).

Oval trinket box

This oval box has been beautifully base painted with a sponge brush in icon green (blue/green); the border has been painted in a specially mixed paprika green. The box has been sanded thoroughly between coats.

The lovely field bouquet consists of Flemish irises, a large rose and rose-bud, blue and white anemones and lilies-of-the-valley (see the pattern on page 13).

The two sides each have a white anemone, rose buds and lilies-of-the-valley. The leaves are mostly medium and dark pine green. The painted designs are protected with two coats of clear gloss. The inside of the box is bright red and monogrammed with the owner's initials. A box like this makes a beautiful gift.

Large oval serving tray with zinnias

In the Northern Hemisphere, July and August are the months for the splendidly artistic zinnias. The pink zinnia is named 'Little William'. I have tried to capture the colours of the beautiful purple, brown, orange/yellow, and Bordeaux red zinnias against the backdrop of the heavenly blue summer sky. The sky blue colour is two parts white paint to one part azure blue; mix thoroughly.

Always sand each base coat well with fine sandpaper. When the surface is very smooth, use a No. 8 brush to make 11 small circles (see page 11). I recommend that you use some retarder medium (e.g. DecoArt) to keep the first layer of paint damp for a time. If necessary, dampen again using an acrylic medium.

Some colour combinations for painting zinnias:
- Begin with a pale yellow/cream circle and build up with blue.
- Try a citrus yellow circle, building this up with a rust red.
- Starting with a totally white circle, build it up with a dusty pink.
- Try an egg yolk yellow circle built up with Bordeaux red.
- Make a light grey circle and build this up with ochre.

The leaves are medium green with a slightly curved yellow edge. The two blue butterflies and the tendrils complete the picture. The centres of the zinnias are not placed straight in the middle of the circles but face in different directions. See the directions on page 11 and the patterns on page 12 for more ideas.

Building up a ranunculus

21

Royal blue and ivory white butler's trays

Butler's trays, document box and English pink serving tray

Butler's trays (opposite page)
These royal blue and ivory white trays belong in a butler's tray stand (available as a complete unit from wood and craft shops). At least three or four base coats were necessary, sanding thoroughly between coats. The royal blue tray was painted in a very traditional manner with a garland of flowers including irises (using the moved tear drop stroke from page 9), roses and tulips (see page 15). A very clear detail of this is shown on the front cover.

The Empire style, another type of folk decoration, can be seen in the ivory tray which includes a traditional bow. The garland is composed from tiger lilies, tulips (both illustrated on page 15), daffodils (illustration page 11), cornflowers (illustration page 6) and ranunculi (illustration page 21). The size of the design is easily adjusted. The pattern will be found inside the back cover.

Document box and English pink serving tray
These two articles have been painted with a crackling medium to give them a wonderful aged effect; this is very fashionable at the moment. The English name for this is weathered wood, but the French call it *craquelé*, (hence the name crackling). On page 29 we will show you how to achieve the crackling effect. You will always need to use two contrasting colours; a light and a dark colour.

For the iris see page 11. You could of course paint the iris white, lilac or purple iris instead of pale blue. This will largely depend on the base colour of the object you are painting.

The serving tray is base painted in an ox-blood (Wacofin or DecoArt). You can create this colour yourself by mixing carmine with a small amount of dark brown or black paint. The crackling was done after the tray had been sanded and thoroughly dried.

For painting the tulip (see page 15), the S stroke and the tear drop stroke (in the centre of the tulip) are made extra wide in this design. Use a very fluid white for the tipping colour. The stem and leaf are also painted extra large. You will need to apply two very large ttt strokes facing in opposite directions to make such a large leaf. Use a No. 10 brush.

Blue document box and English pink serving tray with crackled base coats

Tulip from the English pink serving tray

Tidy box with bluebird, yellow daffodils and violets (see page 26)

Tidy box, pale pink serving tray and wall plaque *(page 26)*

Tidy box
This oval tidy box has been sanded three times and given the same number of coats in ivory white. I mixed a little graphite with the chalk when tracing the pattern (see illustration page 5); this made the pattern easier to see on the light coloured base paint. The pattern is on page 24. This design with its blue bird, yellow daffodils and purple violets has become a big hit with my friends.

It is my interpretation of the first spring walk, when the violets blossom in the woods. Violets abound here in Zwolle, especially where the beech trees grow at the edges of the wood. The right time to find them is the middle of March. The violets are a deep purple/lilac colour and the petals at the top stand straight up.

The bluebird
The method for painting this bright little bluebird is given on page 27. The bird can be painted in three different phases. On page 27 you will also find a closeup of a flying bird which you can use as an alternative. The small feathers in the wing will need to be striped very lightly. See the pattern on page 24.

Pale pink serving tray with decorated edge
This tray has a coral coloured centre on a pale pink background; these are colours from centuries past that are becoming popular again. Mix two parts pastel rose to one part ivory white and you will have a good pale pink base colour. To trace the pattern from page 17, stick the tracing paper down with tape and rub the chalk well into the pores of the paper, following the directions on page 5. The large white summer roses, the blue anemones with buds, the small blue forget-me-nots and the purple violets (see column 3 this page) form a harmonious combination against the coral coloured background (look for 'coral' or 'dusty coral' from DecoArt or FolkArt).

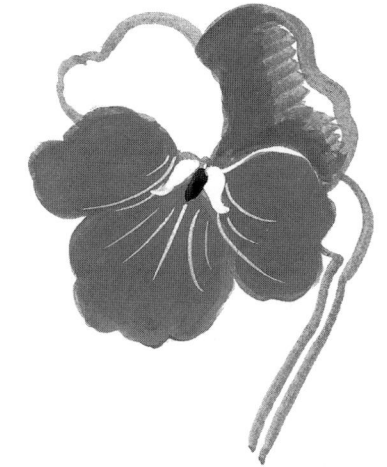

Building up the violet

To paint the tendrils, mix carmine with a dark brown; add some water and mix the paint to a thin consistency, like ink. Use a No. 1 brush or a line brush. Hold the brush vertically and paint the spirals in a circular motion. Lean on your little finger, and remember—practise makes perfect. I recommend that you practise both the roses and the tendrils on a piece of cardboard.

The end result is a very beautiful tray—worth all the hard work!

Wall plaque
This delightful wall plaque in icon green ('mystic green' from FolkArt) with pine green in the centre, displays a bouquet of anemones (see page 16). Anemones, lilies-of-the-valley and two lively bluebirds (see pae 27) form the subject of this composition. If you prefer, you can use a lighter base paint. The anemones are blue, bright red, dark purple, as well as off-white and lilac. All are painted with black stamens in a white centre. The lily-of-the-valley gives an unusual effect against the dark background; the leaves have been painted over the stems of the anemones using ttt strokes, with the four very thin flower stems created using white stem strokes. The little white lily-of-the-valley flowers decrease in size up the stem. This decorative plaque has been coated with two coats of satin sealer.

The purple violet
To paint the violets on the pink serving tray:

A. Two side petals, two top petals, one lower or tongue petal; all painted in one, two or three layers of tear drop strokes.

B. The side petals are painted wet on wet, using white paint. Apply a light edge of ivory white to the top of the petal as well.

C. Make the centre and the stamens using small white and yellow lines and yellow dots.

Butterfly on wall plaque (upper right)

Birds

Building up the bluebird

The bluebird appears on the tidy box, complementing the yellow daffodils and the violets—a true spring scene—and on the wall plaque. If you follow the three steps below you'll find it easy to paint this bird using the simple strokes we already know. A bird is a little more complicated than a flower, but it's not too difficult. Use a No. 4 and a No. 1 or No. 2 brush.

The bluebird
A. Trace the pattern, transferring it onto paper or wood with chalk (see page 5). Paint almost the whole bird white; go over the cheek twice. Add the black eye close to the beak. The upper part of the wing is coloured with a little green and brown paint.

B. Using a No. 1 brush, make the eye into a circle and add a small white dot. Using small flat comma strokes and mid blue paint begin the tail, the lower part of the wing and the shoulder from bottom to top. Make a C stroke above the cheek from the beak to the back, using the same blue. The upper wing and the shoulder are blue toward the front, and moss green toward the back. The breast (to above the tail), is bright yellow with a little ochre shaded along the wing.

C. Mix mid blue with white to make sky blue and add some of this colour to the head and wings (see the example on this page). Make a 'bar' of fine white stripes slightly above the centre of the wing.
  Add a small amount of black to a No. 1 brush; dab a row of small grey/black dots wet on wet around the cheek and from the centre of the cheek to the eye. Lighten the breast with a little white. Dry the brush with your fingers and lightly mix the green and blue at the top of the wing. A row of white dots finishes the wing.

< *Tidy box, pale pink serving tray and icon-shaped wall plaque. (See pages 24–25)*

Close-up of the fluttering bluebird from the wall plaque (page 26)

The red robin (male and female)
A. Trace the pattern for the chest of drawers (pages 28, 30, 31) with chalk and tracing paper. Paint the base for the bird completely in white. Using a No. 4 and a No. 1 brush, mix mid-brown with some ochre and add a little grey to create a light brown colour. Paint the back, the wing, the tail and the top of the head. The breast is painted either with sienna or a mixture of ochre and orange. When this mix is partly dry, squeeze the brush between your fingers; using the brush, blend both colours together to achieve a soft even balance between the brown and the orange.

B. Accentuate the points of the wing and the head with a dark brown (not too dark) tint. Place in the eye, then darken the beak and the end of the wing. Work neatly and carefully. You can effectively create the wing feathers by using a No. 1 brush and painting very fine white lines on the wing.

C. The female robin is slightly larger than her mate; she is turning back to look at the male bird. The colouring for both is very similar. The feet have three small black claws. On a mid-grey base paint, these red robins will stand out smartly.

Building up the red robins, as they appear on pages 30–31

27

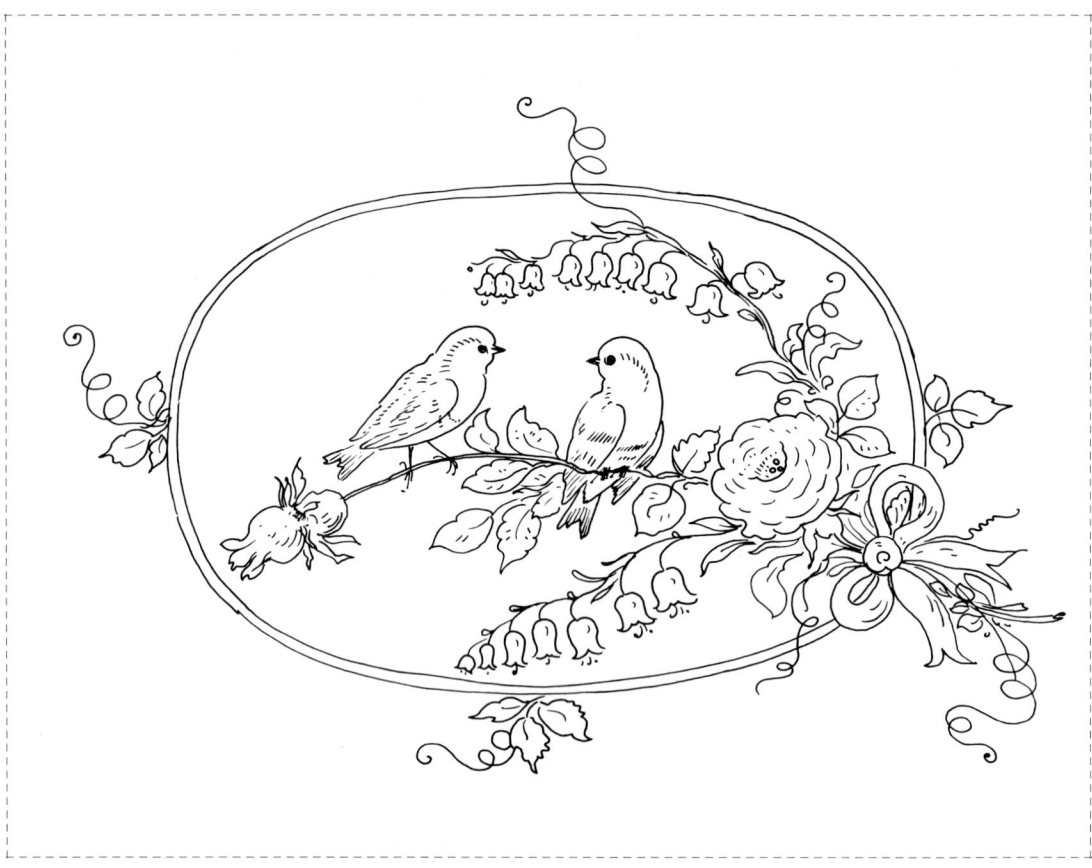

A. Top of red robin chest of drawers (see page 30)

B. Top and bottom drawers for red robin chest of drawers (see page 30)

C. Middle drawer from red robin chest of drawers (see page 30)

The pattern for the side panel of the chest of drawers is inside the front cover

Crackling and antiquing

Crackling

There are several different ways to apply crackle; some are more costly than others and the degrees of complexity vary.

I have chosen to use a squeeze bottle of crackling medium available from DecoArt and FolkArt. Read the instructions before using them. Always use rubber gloves; direct contact with your skin and eyes can cause irritation, so take care.

The article has to be base coated with a dark coloured acrylic-base paint (dark brown, carmine, dark green or dark blue, for example). This base coat needs to be smooth, dust free and dry.

Step 1: With a wide flat hogshair brush, apply one coat of crackle over the base coat. This will need 20 to 30 minutes to dry; make sure to follow the manufacturer's instructions. Brush on the crackle in one direction only (see photo).

Step 2: The contrasting lighter coloured paint needs to be well mixed and fluid. Use light ochre, pale pink, light green or off white with any of the above-named base colours. The flat brush must be totally covered in crackling medium. Apply the paint in one long stroke; make your second stroke directly next to the first, and your third stroke next to your second, and so on. This will ensure a nice even crackle pattern. Do not make half strokes and avoid brushing over the same stroke twice, as you will not get an even crackle pattern this way.

Hint: on page 23 pale pink was painted over oxblood for the tray, and on the box a light grey blue was painted over a very dark blue. Always use two contrasting colours; you can also use very dark coloured paint over a pale colour. This very old decorative method is extremely effective.

Antiquing

This decorative technique gives objects an aged and weathered look. The word is actually of French origin. Any object that is completely dry can be antiqued and, provided it is done correctly, the surface will be given an antique appearance.

I have seen German folk artists rub off the antiquing medium (patina) with steel wool after leaving their articles to dry for two days. We will use a simpler method. Oil-based patina is available as well as a water-soluble one. I have used the latter.

Step 1: Pour a small amount of brown patina (a mixture of two browns is also possible), into a dish or plate. Using a piece of cotton or tricot cloth, apply a little pressure and rub the patina onto the plate in a circular motion.

Step 2: If you have not used patina before, you can add a small amount of acrylic medium to prevent it drying out too quickly. If that doesn't allow you enough time, apply a little extender to increase the drying time; however, this will make your patina more transparent.

The water-based patina is not left to dry on the object. Most of it is wiped carefully away with a clean cloth, until you have the desired effect. The drying time is approximately 1 to 2 hours.

If you wish to lighten certain details, such as the white cheek of a bird, wrap the cloth around your finger and rub thoroughly.

Remember that the more patina you apply to the object, the more you will need to rub off; use small amounts.

Personally, I prefer the antique finish created with the oil-based patina. It allows me more time to highlight parts of the design by rubbing. The process is very similar to that descibed above but the drying time is at least 48 hours, which makes a big difference. You can use a quick drying oil paint medium or Liquin from Winsor & Newton to help you achieve an even coating; this method allows the patina to be applied with a brush, especially on large objects or furniture.

After allowing the object to dry for 48 to 72 hours, you can apply a coat of matt sealer over the antiqued surface.

Crackle phase 1: the crackle medium is applied with a flat brush

Crackle phase 2: applying the second colour, stroke by stroke; do not paint over the same area again

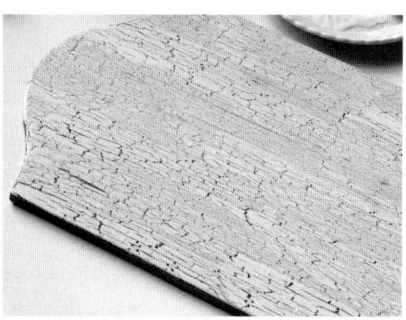

Crackle phase 3: drying—the first cracks are starting to show

Antiquing: Rub the patina all over the object, using a circular action

Crackled chest of drawers with red robins

Red robins

This charming piece of furniture would suit a hallway, landing or living room.

After the chest of drawers had been thoroughly sanded, it was given a base coat of ochre yellow and another coat of light gold acrylic (bronze). When the base coats were dry, the chest was crackled one surface at a time; the drawers were done last. The very fluid white paint was applied stroke by stroke. Once the crackling medium dried, the grey/green medallions were painted with a sponge applicator. Following that, the patterns with the red robins, roses, honeysuckle and bluebells were transferred to the chest. All the motifs have been demonstrated in colour, except for the bluebells. The bluebell is quite simple; it is painted using a wet on wet technique with a light and a dark side.

The medallion trim is two coats of carmine; the second coat has been mixed with a little metallic paint. The bow is painted in a 19th century Biedermeier style. The white rose has touches of ochre and carmine worked into it. The side panel of the chest of drawers shows only the male robin, while the oval scene on the top has both the female and male birds sitting on the same rose twig.

These designs are all very suitable for door panels, butler's trays, boxes and serving trays. The patterns all appear on page 28, except for the side panel—this is found on the inside front cover.

< Side panel from chest of drawers; male robin amidst flower bouquet

Blue bells

> Top of chest of drawers: both robins on a rose twig

31

Finishing off, cleaning and maintenance

Finishing off and varnishing

What else do you need to do to your work? In most cases one or two coats of clear varnish are sufficient to guard the article from wear and tear. This protection is particularly important for boxes because they are constantly being opened and closed.

Water-soluble and turpentine-based varnishes are available in gloss, satin and matte finishes. Hobbyists mostly use the satin varnish. Water-soluble varnishes are environmentally friendly and the brushes you use can be washed with water and detergent.

Small objects like wooden frames, albums, note books and the like, only need one coat of varnish. They need at least one day to dry properly. When an article has been antiqued, you will need to make sure that it is completely dry before using two coats of varnish to seal it. Make sure you read the directions for drying times.

If you are painting flower bouquets on handmade paper, apply a layer of acrylic medium with a sponge brush before you start to paint. This creates a very good base on which to paint. When the painting is finished it can be given a layer of protective spray to help prevent both the paper and paint yellowing.

Cleaning and maintenance

If a piece of furniture has been properly coated with varnish, you can clean it simply by wiping it with a wet cloth. Never use harsh chemical abrasives or detergents on your varnished objects. This could dissolve the sealer and eventually affect the decorative painting. After a while a piece of furniture can be brightened up with another coat of varnish. This should be done in a dust-free area.

If you wish to learn more about classic folk art finishes on furniture, look for relevant books at your library.

I hope this book has given you an insight into the art of Assendelfter painting and increases your pleasure in pursuing the hobby.

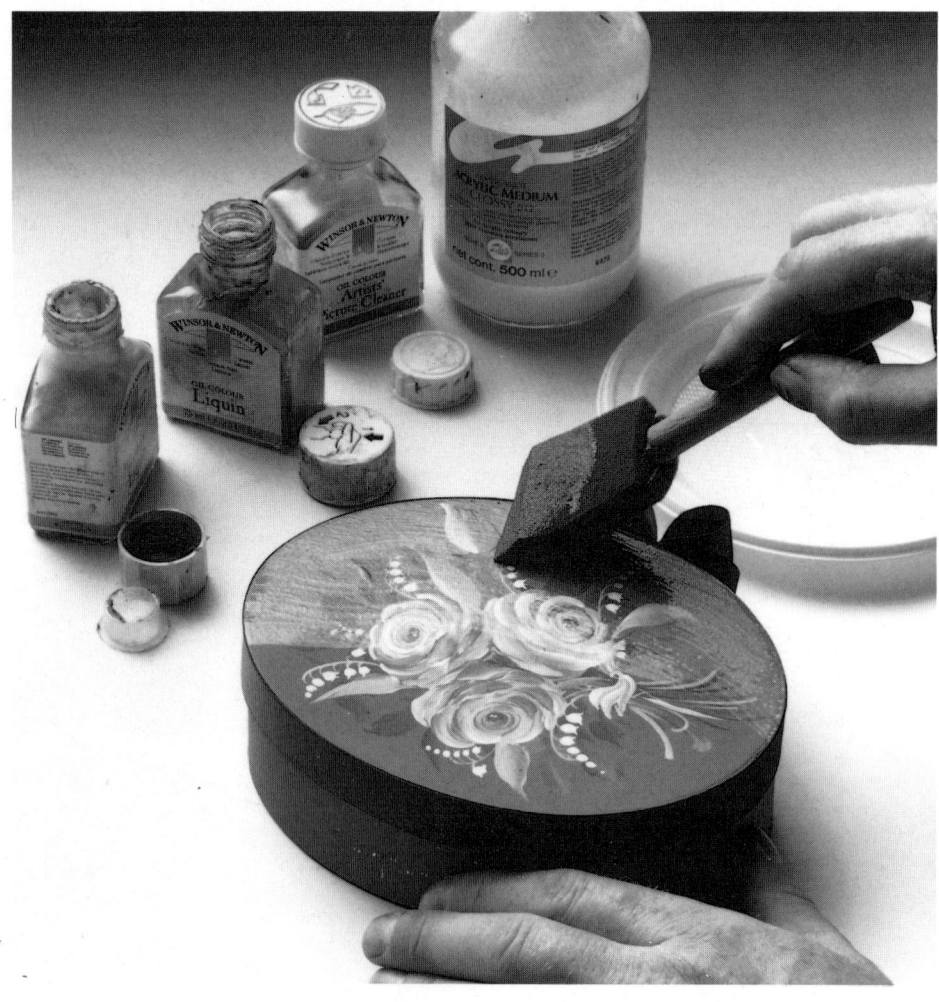

A Spanish box is given a coat of varnish with a sponge applicator